DANCE ★ CRAZY

Samba
& Lambada

DANCE ★ CRAZY

Samba
& Lambada

Paul Bottomer

LORENZ BOOKS

This edition published by Lorenz Books

© 1997 Anness Publishing Limited

Lorenz Books is an imprint of
Anness Publishing Limited
Hermes House
88–89 Blackfriars Road
London SE1 8HA

ISBN 1 85967 395 3

A CIP catalogue record for this book is available from the British Library.

Publisher: Joanna Lorenz
Senior Editor: Lindsay Porter
Photographer: John Freeman
Clothes Stylist: Leeann Mackenzie
Hair and Make-up: Karen Kennedy
Designer: Siân Keogh

Printed in China

3 5 7 9 10 8 6 4 2

Contents

Samba – an Introduction

The Portuguese explorers who first sailed along the coast of South America one January morning discovered the beauty of a series of bays with golden beaches, fed by a fresh river running through lush tropical peaks. When they named that idyllic spot "January River", or Rio de Janeiro in Portuguese, they could hardly have imagined what the future had in store. Portuguese colonists settled and, as agriculture prospered, slaves were brought from the Portuguese-controlled areas of south-west Africa to work in the plantations of Bahia, in the north-east of what would later become Brazil. Samba began to develop in the Bahia region as a response to the strong percussive rhythms of a type of drums called "Batuque", which the slaves had brought with them from Africa. The hypnotic beat of the "Batuque" enabled the early Samba dancers to escape for a while from their everyday troubles and dance barefoot, a tradition still upheld today in the Samba de Roda. In the language of those slaves, the word for dance was "Semba", a word that was destined to pass into the folklore of Brazil as the proud name of the national dance.

Now the Samba is the dance of celebration and joy at the Carnival held in Rio each February. The Carnival Samba dancers vie with each other as to who can wear the most enormous and fabulous headdresses which make all but the most basic foot movements impossible. This kind of Samba is very different from the more stylized international version. In Rio, the Samba is danced solo whereas the international Samba is a dance for couples. To a rhythm of "Quick, Quick, Slow &", the Rio dancers perform fast three-step weight changes with a slight knee lift, the sections of which are led with alternate feet. The women are adept at showing off their hip movements while the men's action is less exaggerated. Meanwhile, the head is kept perfectly still to avoid toppling the magnificent edifice it is supporting. The Samba as a dance for couples is also popular in Brazil and a slower version, called the Pagode (pronounced pa-go-day), is enjoyed for social purposes.

Left: Smart, casual clothes are best for dancing the Samba. Women should wear short dresses for ease of movement, as well as shoes with a heel. Men should choose shoes with a good sole – rubber-soled shoes are not suitable.

The Maxixe (pronounced ma-shee-shay) was the first version of the Samba to become known outside Brazil and gained some popularity in Europe, although that dwindled during the First World War. By the late 1930s, however, the catchy, carefree, fun-loving Samba was enthralling dancers in the United States and during the late 1930s and 1940s, both Rio and its Samba were capturing the imagination of the masses through the medium of cinema. Carmen Miranda featured in many Hollywood films, forging the popular archetypal images of Brazil and the Samba. Fred Astaire and Ginger Rogers further popularized the idea of Rio as an exotic, romantic and sophisticated backdrop to the dance in the motion picture *Flying Down to Rio* and the Samba flourished around the world.

When the popularity of a dance transports it beyond the boundaries of its own traditional and cultural context, it is natural that it will develop in a more international style. If such changes take place within the original character and spirit of the dance, then the result can enrich the dance, making it more varied and

internationally appealing. Although inappropriate fad styles are sometimes applied to the Samba, as in the disco look given to the dance in the 1970s or the sharp, staccato feel of the 1990s these tend not to stand the test of time and fade in favour of an approach which embraces the dance's original character.

For many social dancers, their local Latin American club, restaurant or bar is the place to relax, meet friends and dance the Samba. At these clubs, the music tends to be more authentically Brazilian, with dance moves taking on a more spontaneous and improvisational style. This book, though, will describe simplified versions of standard figures in the international style of Samba which is quite different from the Samba danced by Carnival-goers in Rio. It is taught by officially recognized dance teachers throughout the world and not only ensures compatibility of moves between dancers from different countries, but also provides a logical, structured and easily understandable approach to learning the Samba.

Right: The dramatic, energetic Samba is danced by couples not only in Brazil, but all over the world.

On the Floor

In the international Standard Dances, such as the Waltz and Quickstep, couples move around the dance floor in an overall anticlockwise direction. In some internationally standardized Latin American dances, such as the Mambo, Cha Cha Cha or the Rumba, couples generally do not progress around the floor but dance occupying only a small area of the floor. In the Samba, however, some moves remain relatively stationary, while others progress around the room. To learn the pattern of the figures and to move comfortably around the floor, with consideration for the other dancers, you will first need to become accustomed to orientating yourself in the room.

GOING WITH THE FLOW

Assuming that the room is rectangular, the man stands facing the wall and the woman stands backing the wall. To progress with the flow of floor traffic as it moves anticlockwise around the room, the man moves to his left and the woman to her right. The line of flow runs around the floor, parallel with the wall.

THE CENTRE LINE

With the couple still in the same position, the room's centre line runs parallel to the wall, behind the man and in front of the woman.

Right: Floorcraft adds to your dancing pleasure.

CORNERING

In the Samba, you may choose to dance a particular figure to help you move from one wall to the next. But mostly, you will simply curve the figures as necessary when you reach a corner of the room. Care should be taken not to distort the figures too much and make them difficult or uncomfortable to dance. Once you have negotiated the corner, you will need to re-orientate yourself along the new wall.

Basic Floorcraft

While you are dancing around the floor, you should try to be aware of other dancers and their likely direction of travel. The ability to avoid problems is a great asset to a dancer and ways of doing this are highlighted later in the book. There are, however, a few general rules which are worth mentioning at this point.

• It makes sense for more experienced dancers to give way to less experienced dancers.
• Whoever can see a potential problem should take avoiding action. This is usually the couple who are further back in the flow of floor traffic.
• Less experienced dancers and dancers who progress more slowly around the floor should follow a path near to the wall so as not to impede more experienced and quicker dancers.
• Never dance across the centre line of the room into the oncoming flow of floor traffic.

With practice, the ability to avoid problems will itself become an enjoyable feature of your dancing.

Music and Rhythm

The euphoric excitement of the Carnival effervesces through the surging rhythms and vivacious melodies of the Samba to bring a party atmosphere to any occasion. The speed, or tempo, of the Samba can vary quite dramatically from 48–52 bars per minute for social dancing, through 53 bars per minute for examinations and competitions, up to 58 bars per minute for very fast Brazilian Sambas. The variety of percussive instruments available to musicians in the Samba's native Brazil has led to a multiplicity of rhythms, each of which echoes the dance's origins in south-west Africa and has its own special accent and feel. The time signature of the Samba is generally 2/4, which means that the rhythm has two counts to one bar of music with a value of four beats (i.e. two beats to each count), or 4/4, which means four counts to one bar. The Samba moves and figures have different rhythms and you will become accustomed to these with time.

For the purposes of this book, we will assume that the time signature is 2/4. If this is difficult to understand, don't worry. Many of the fantastic Brazilian musicians have no technical knowledge of the rhythms they are producing yet can still make music which is pure South American magic. It is not necessary to think consciously about

Right: Enjoy the beat of the Samba and Lambada.

the beat values while you are dancing, although an appreciation of the nature of the rhythms will help you to understand the figures.

Each step of the figures in the book will be given a count. Using the 2/4 time signature, the value of each count will be one of the following:

Slow = 1 beat or Quick = ½ beat.

The beat will frequently be split to provide exciting rhythmic combinations. The split beats are conventionally described as:

& = ½ beat or a = ¼ beat.

When the beat is split, the smaller, quicker fraction of the beat is taken from the preceding beat. In the count of 1 a 2, the "a" count is taken from the preceding "1" count, so that the "1" count is only ¾ of a beat and not a whole beat.

Examples:

Count	Beat value
1 a 2	¾ ¼ 1
Slow a Slow	¾ ¼ 1
1 a 2 a 3 a 4	¾ ¼ ¾ ¼ ¾ ¼ 1
Slow a Slow	
a Slow a Slow	¾ ¼ ¾ ¼ ¾ ¼ 1
Slow Quick Quick	1 ½ ½
Quick Quick Slow	½ ½ 1

When the music has a 4/4 time signature, the beat values given above are doubled.

The Dance Floor

As the dance floor is primarily for the benefit of the dancers, it should not be used as a thoroughfare. Always walk around the edge of the floor and never across it. The sudden emergence of a bystander trying to dodge dancing couples can cause chaos and is an unnecessary hazard to the dancers. When taking to the floor, avoid causing any problems for the dancers who are already there. Since men will normally start the dance facing the outside of the room, it may seem natural for them to walk on to the floor backwards with their attention focused on their partner. As they will not easily be able to avoid dancers in this position, it is far better to approach the floor and assess the flow of floor traffic before taking up a starting position with due consideration to the other dancers.

When leaving the floor, especially during a dance, the same consideration should be shown. Dance to the edge of the floor and leave it at that point. Drinks should never be carried across the floor, as spills can cause sticky or slippery patches which are dangerous to dancers and difficult to clean up. Smoking on the floor is totally unacceptable.

WHICH FOOT TO START WITH AND WHY

Some dance schools advocate starting the dance with a move called the Natural Basic Movement which starts with the man moving his right foot forward, or the Reverse Basic Movement in which the man moves his left foot forward. Either are in theory correct. However, if the man can move forward with either foot but without a turn, it is impossible for the woman to tell which foot he intends to use. For this reason, the best start to the dance is to use the Side Basic Samba or a Samba Whisk (see the next section) in which the man moves sideways and is able much more easily to communicate his intention to his partner.

Left: Consideration for other dancers is vital dance-floor etiquette.

The Hold

In different Samba figures, different holds will be used which give variety to the shape and feel of the dance. These various holds will be described as you progress through the figures in the book. At the start of the dance, it is sensible for the man to choose a simple hold which offers him the best contact with the woman in order to lead her into their first move. Most social dancers therefore start in a Close Hold.

CLOSE HOLD

The man and woman stand a little apart and square to each other. The man's right hand cups the woman's left shoulder-blade while she rests her left hand lightly on his right upper arm or shoulder, so that her arm follows the same curve as the man's. With his left elbow at the same height as his right elbow, the man raises his left hand to just below eye level and takes the woman's right hand. His left arm should be curved gently forward so that his hand is on a line running between the couple. The man

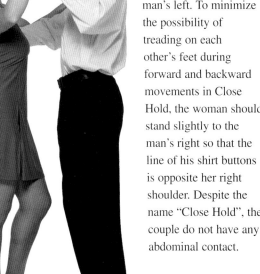

takes hold by presenting his left hand to the woman as if he were a policeman stopping traffic. His thumb should extend naturally to the side. The woman then hooks her middle finger on to the man's hand between his thumb and fingers, palm to palm. She lowers her second and fourth fingers over her middle finger and then lowers her little finger. She wraps her thumb around the base of the man's thumb and the man closes his fingers around the woman's hand. The woman's right arm matches the curve of the man's left. To minimize the possibility of treading on each other's feet during forward and backward movements in Close Hold, the woman should stand slightly to the man's right so that the line of his shirt buttons is opposite her right shoulder. Despite the name "Close Hold", the couple do not have any abdominal contact.

Left: The Close Hold, seen from two angles.

Basic Samba

While you are still beginning to accustom yourself to the speed, rhythm and action of the Samba, it is a good idea to start the dance with an easy move. Start in Close Hold, with the man facing the wall and the woman facing the centre line of the room. Your feet should be together, the man standing with his weight on the left foot and the woman with her weight on the right foot.

SIDE BASIC SAMBA TO THE RIGHT

1 Man
Move sideways on to the right foot.
(Count – slow)

2 Man
Close the left foot to the right foot. (a)

3 Man
Transfer
your
body
weight on
to the
right
foot.
(Count –
slow)

1 Woman
Move sideways on to the left foot.
(Count – slow)

2 Woman
Close the right foot to the left foot. (a)

3
Woman
Transfer your body
weight on to the left foot. (Count – slow)

> ## Rhythm Tip
>
> As you dance the Side Basic Samba, you might like to reinforce the rhythm by saying to yourself, "Step. Change feet".

SIDE BASIC SAMBA TO THE LEFT

1 Man

Move sideways on to the left foot.
(Count – slow)

2 Man

Close the right foot to the left foot. (a)

3 Man

Transfer your body weight on to the left foot. (Count – slow)

1 Woman

Move sideways on to the right foot.
(Count – slow)

2 Woman

Close the left foot to the right foot. (a)

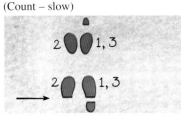
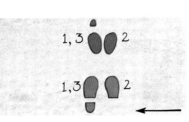

3 Woman

Transfer your body weight on to the right foot. (Count – slow)

Samba Action

Once you have learned the simple pattern of the Side Basic Samba, you will want to practise it a few times continuously. As you do this, you can start to introduce the all-important Samba action which gives the dance its unique feel.

2 Man and Woman
As you dance Step 2, straighten the knees a little but do not lower the heel on to the floor.

3 Man and Woman
Relax down (ball–flat) again into Step 3.

1 Man and Woman
Start with both knees a little flexed. As you start the move to the side, straighten the knees. As you put your weight on to the moving foot, lower from the ball of the foot on to the flat foot and flex knees to end the first count.

This action is known as the "Samba Bounce Action" but you must be careful not to exaggerate it: it should be a gentle, rhythmic action felt through the knees and ankles. The Samba Bounce Action will be used in some of the other figures in the book.

Samba Whisk

The Samba Whisk is a very useful basic figure which uses the Samba Bounce Action to full advantage. Start in Close Hold with the man facing the wall and the woman facing the centre line of the room. The man is standing with his weight on the left foot and the woman with her weight on the right foot.

SAMBA WHISK TO THE RIGHT

1 Man
Move sideways on to the right foot (ball–flat). (Count – slow)

1 Woman
Move sideways on to the left foot (ball–flat). (Count – slow)

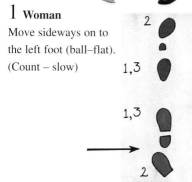

2 Man
Cross the left foot behind the right foot with the toes of the left foot just behind the heel of the right foot and turned out a little. Flex both knees. Allow the right heel to lift momentarily from the floor as you stand on the toes of the left foot. (a)

2 Woman
Cross the right foot behind the left foot, with the toes of the right foot just behind the heel of the left foot and turned out a little. Flex both knees. Allow the left heel to lift momentarily from the floor as you stand on the toes of the right foot. (a)

3 Man
Lower your body weight on to the right foot (ball–flat). (Count – slow)

3 Woman
Lower your body weight on to the left foot (ball–flat). (Count – slow)

SAMBA WHISK TO THE LEFT

1 Man

Move sideways on to the left foot (ball–flat). (Count – slow)

1 Woman

Move sideways on to the right foot (ball–flat). (Count – slow)

2 Man

Cross the right foot behind the left foot, with the toes of the right foot just behind the heel of the left foot and turned out a little. Flex both knees. Allow the left heel to lift momentarily from the floor as you stand on the toes of the right foot. (a)

2 Woman

Cross the left foot behind the right foot, with the toes of the left foot just behind the heel of the right foot and turned out a little. Flex both knees. Allow the right heel to lift momentarily from the floor as you stand on the toes of the left foot. (a)

3 Man

Lower your body weight on to the left foot (ball–flat). (Count – slow)

3 Woman

Lower your body weight on to the right foot (ball–flat). (Count – slow)

Footwork

Footwork refers to the part of the foot used in contact with the floor during a step. Dancers often note footwork using abbreviations.

B = ball of the foot
F = flat foot
T = toe

In the Samba Whisk, the footwork is therefore: 1. BF, 2. T, 3. BF.

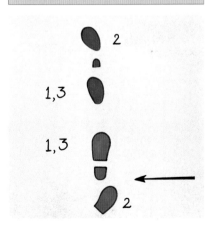

Samba Steps

LATIN CROSS

Crossing the feet in Step 2 of the Whisk is called the Latin Cross. It may be danced in some figures as a cross in front.

STEP IN PLACE

At the end of Step 3 of the Samba Whisk the foot is in the same position as at the start of the step. This is known as a "Step in Place".

TAKING A STEP

When taking a step, remember that you not only move your foot into position but also move your body weight on to that foot. This is particularly crucial in the Samba where the body will need to move into position to be ready for a possible weight change on a split beat.

PART WEIGHT

This term is applied to a step with an "a" or an "&" count, where the body weight is transferred on to the foot, but only for a moment, while the other foot takes up its new position.

Promenade Position

In the Promenade Position, the dancers assume a different position relative to each other. In Promenade Position, the distance between the man's left side and the woman's right side is greater than the distance between the man's right side and the woman's left side. This means that the couple will be more "open" on the man's left and the woman's right side. The actual amount by which they open up depends on the requirements of the particular figure to be danced.

As a result of moving into this position, the man lowers his left hand slightly and allows his right hand to slide a little more around the woman's back. The woman moves her left hand correspondingly around the back of the man's shoulder.

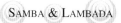
Samba Walks in Promenade Position

So far, you have been dancing the Side Basic Samba and the Samba Whisk in a stationary position. The Samba Walks will allow you to move steadily forwards with the flow along the room. The Samba Walks are danced in Promenade Position, so you will need to modify the Samba Whisk to end in the correct starting position for this figure. First dance a Samba Whisk to the Right, then a Samba Whisk to the Left and then another to the Right. On the final Samba Whisk to the Right, the man turns 90° to his left (anticlockwise) and the woman 90° to her right (clockwise) to end facing with the flow in Promenade Position. The man is standing with his weight on the right foot and the woman with her weight on the left foot.

LEFT FOOT SAMBA WALK

1 Man

Move forward a small step, on to the left foot, moving with the flow and ending with your hips over your foot. Allow the right knee to close towards the left knee. (Count – slow)

1 Woman

Move forward a small step, on to the right foot, moving with the flow and ending with your hips over your foot. Allow the left knee to close towards the right knee. (Count – slow)

Footwork

1. BF, 2. B (inside edge), 3. F

Style Tip

A little Samba Bounce Action is used on the Samba Walks, so you should feel a slight rocking movement as you dance this figure.

2 Man

Extend the right foot back (part weight). (a)

2 Woman

Extend the left foot back (part weight). (a)

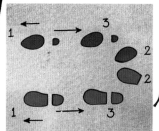

3 Man

Slip the left foot back underneath your body. (Count – slow)

3 Woman

Slip the right foot back underneath your body. (Count – slow)

Now repeat the Samba Walk. This time the man starts with his right foot and the woman with her left.

Basic Samba: Short Routine

With the moves you have already learned, you can now dance a short basic routine.

• Samba Whisk to the Right, Left and Right, ending in Promenade Position
• Left Foot Samba Walk, Right Foot Samba Walk
• Left Foot Samba Walk, Right Foot Samba Walk
• Samba Whisk to the Left, turned 90° to the right (clockwise) for the man, to end facing the wall, and 90° to the left (anti-clockwise) for the woman, to end facing the centre line
• Start again from the beginning

RIGHT FOOT SAMBA WALK

1 Man

Move forward a small step, on to the right foot, moving with the flow and ending with your hips over your foot. Allow the left knee to close towards the right knee. (Count – slow)

1 Woman

Move forward a small step, on to the left foot, moving with the flow and ending with your hips over your foot. Allow the right knee to close towards the left knee. (Count – slow)

2 Man

Extend the left foot back (part weight). (a)

2 Woman

Extend the right foot back (part weight). (a)

3 Man

Slip the right foot back underneath your body. (Count – slow)

3 Woman

Slip the left foot back underneath your body. (Count – slow)

Footwork

1. BF, 2. B (inside edge), 3. F

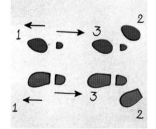

You can now repeat the Samba Walks in Promenade Position, starting them with alternate feet.

Side Samba Walk

S ome Samba figures are joined together by inserting a linking move. The Side Samba Walk is a modified version of the figure you have just learned and will enable you to progress into the next classic Samba figure – the Volta. Start having just danced a Left Foot Samba Walk in Promenade Position. The man is now standing on the left foot and the woman on the right foot. The couple is in Promenade Position, facing with the flow. A slight Samba Bounce Action is used in this figure.

1 Man
Move forward a small step, on to the right foot, moving with the flow and ending with your hips over your foot. Allow the left knee to close towards the right knee. (Count – slow)

1 Woman
Move forward a small step, on to the left foot, moving with the flow and ending with your hips over your foot. Allow the right knee to close towards the left knee. (Count – slow)

2 Man
Making a 45° turn to the right, extend the left foot to the side (part weight). (a)

2 Woman
Making a 45° turn to the left, extend the right foot to the side (part weight). (a)

3 Man
Slip the right foot to the left underneath your body. You have ended in Open Promenade Position. (Count – slow)

3 Woman
Slip the left foot to the right underneath your body. You have ended in Open Promenade Position. (Count – slow)

Footwork
1.BF, 2.B (inside edge), 3. F

Continue with the Travelling Volta or the Bota Fogos in Shadow Position.

Travelling Voltas

The Volta is a Samba move which is so full of vibrant rhythm and colour it has become a classic figure in the Samba repertoire. The Volta's popularity has led it to be adapted to be danced in a wide variety of interesting and enjoyable ways. In this version, the man's and woman's paths cross over each other as they progress along the floor in the Travelling Volta. This move extends the "Slow a Slow" rhythm across two bars of music and is conventionally counted as "1 a 2 a 3 a 4". Start having just danced the Side Samba Walk. The man is standing on the right foot and the woman on the left foot in Open Promenade Position. The man is holding the woman's right hand in his left. The Samba Bounce Action is used throughout this figure and the body weight is focused over the front foot.

TRAVELLING VOLTA TO THE RIGHT

Man Dance a gentle curve first towards the wall, then to the left to end facing the centre line of the room. The left and right feet will travel the path of the figure in parallel lines. At the start of the move, lift the left hand to allow the woman to pass under your arm and in front of you. When the woman has passed, you can return the hand to its normal position. Start with the left foot, which will remain in front.

Woman Dance a gentle curve first towards the centre line, then to the right to end facing the wall. The right and left feet will travel the path of the figure in parallel lines. During the move, the man will raise your hand to allow you to pass under his arm and in front of him. Start with the right foot, which will remain in front.

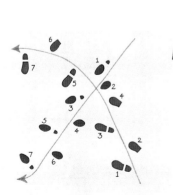

1 Man
Move the left foot across, in front of the right foot and along the curve (Latin Cross). (Count – slow – 1)

1 Woman
Move the right foot across, in front of the left foot and along the curve (Latin Cross). (Count – slow – 1)

2 Man

Move the right foot sideways a short step along the curve (part weight). (a)

3 Man

Move the left foot across, in front of the right foot and along the curve (Latin Cross). (Count – slow – 2)

3 Woman

Move the right foot across, in front of the left foot and along the curve (Latin Cross). (Count – slow – 2)

4 Man

Move the right foot sideways a short step along the curve (part weight). (a)

4 Woman

Move the left foot sideways a short step along the curve (part weight). (a)

5 Man

Repeat step 3. (Count – slow – 3)

5 Woman

Repeat step 3. (Count – slow – 3)

6 Man

Repeat step 4 (part weight). (a)

6 Woman

Repeat step 4 (part weight). (a)

7 Man

Move the left foot across, in front of the right foot and along the curve to end facing the centre line (Latin Cross). (Count – slow – 4)

7 Woman

Move the right foot across, in front of the left foot and along the curve to end facing the wall (Latin Cross). (Count – slow – 4)

2 Woman

Move the left foot sideways a short step along the curve (part weight). (a)

Footwork

1. BF, 2. T, 3. BF, 4. T, 5. BF, 6. T, 7. BF

You can now continue with the Travelling Volta to the Left.

22

TRAVELLING VOLTA TO THE LEFT

Man Dance a gentle curve first towards the centre line, then to the right to end facing the wall. The right and left feet will travel the path of the figure in parallel lines. At the start of the move, lift the left hand to allow the woman to pass under your arm and in front of you. When the woman has passed, you can return the hand to its normal position. Start with the right foot, which will remain in front, and focus your body weight over this foot.

Woman Dance a gentle curve first towards the wall, then to the left to end facing the centre line. The left and right feet will travel the path of the figure in parallel lines. During the move, the man will raise your hand to allow you to pass under his arm and in front of him. Start with the left foot, which will remain in front, and focus your body weight over this foot.

Footwork

1. BF, 2. T, 3. BF, 4. T, 5. BF, 6. T, 7. BF

1 Man
Move the right foot across, in front of the left foot, and along the curve (Latin Cross). (Count – slow – 1)

1 Woman
Move the left foot across, in front of the right foot, and along the curve (Latin Cross). (Count – slow – 1)

2 Man
Move the left foot sideways a short step along the curve (part weight). (a)

2 Woman
Move the right foot sideways a short step along the curve (part weight). (a)

3 Man
Move the right foot across, in front of the left foot, and along the curve (Latin Cross). (Count – slow – 2)

3 Woman
Move the left foot across, in front of the right foot, and along the curve (Latin Cross). (Count – slow

23

4 Man

Move the left foot sideways a short step along the curve (part weight). (a)

4 Woman

Move the right foot sideways a short step along the curve (part weight). (a)

5 Man

Move the right foot across, in front of the left foot and along the curve (Latin Cross). (Count – slow – 3)

5 Woman

Move the left foot across, in front of the right foot and along the curve (Latin Cross). (Count – slow – 3)

6 Man

Move the left foot sideways a short step along the curve (part weight). (a)

6 Woman

Move the right foot sideways a short step along the curve (part weight). (a)

7 Man

Move the right foot across, in front of the left foot and along the curve to end facing the wall (Latin Cross). (Count – slow – 4)

7 Woman

Move the left foot across, in front of the right foot and along the curve to end facing the centre line (Latin Cross). (Count – slow – 4)

Action Tip

For both the man and the woman, it is important that the body weight is held forward over the front foot during the Travelling Voltas, with only sufficient weight moving over the back foot to allow the front foot to progress. The lowering (ball–flat) on to the front foot and the rising (toe) on to the back foot should not be exaggerated and you should not feel more than a suggestion of up and down movement through the Samba Bounce Action. The body should remain upright and over your front foot. Take small steps, as they are not only more comfortable but very much more stylish.

Having danced the Travelling Voltas to the Left and to the Right, you are now in a position to continue back into your routine, starting with the Samba Whisk to the Left.

What to Do with the Free Arm

In the Samba, there are many moves requiring a hold with only one hand. By following some general guidelines about what to do with your free arm and hand, you can give your dance a superb appearance and a balanced feel.

• In social dancing, the free arm should never be held above shoulder height. There is no good reason to do so and it makes the dancer look shorter.

• The free arm should never be dropped to the side as this severely inhibits good balance.

position mirroring the joined hand and arm.

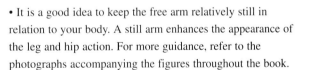

• As you develop a feel for the dance, you may wish to respond by moving the free arm in a natural, balanced and gentle way.

• Do not exaggerate the movements and match not only your own movements but also those of your partner.

• It is a good idea to keep the free arm relatively still in relation to your body. A still arm enhances the appearance of the leg and hip action. For more guidance, refer to the photographs accompanying the figures throughout the book.

• In a travelling move, the position of the free hand and arm should mirror the height and curve of the joined hand and arm. The fingers of the free hand can be held either all together with the thumb extended or with the third and fourth fingers lowered slightly to give a more "Latin" look.

• During a turn on the spot, the arm should be drawn out of the way across the body and then allowed to return naturally to its

Leg and Hip Action

Much is talked about the Samba hip action, yet an appropriate hip action is really only the by-product of a good leg, knee and ankle action. The Samba Bounce Action has already been described in detail, and "Action Tips" accompany the figures which use a different type of action.

Bota Fogos in Shadow Position

Bota Fogo (pronounced boat-a-foe-go) is a neighbourhood in the beautiful city of Rio de Janeiro and it was after this part of the city that your next figure was named. The Bota Fogos, like the Voltas, have become a classic figure essential to the character of the Samba. You can now insert the Bota Fogos in Shadow Position between the Side Samba Walk and the Travelling Volta to the Right. During the Bota Fogos, the man retains hold with the left hand while the woman dances her Bota Fogos across and in front of him. A slight Samba Bounce Action is used throughout. This figure progresses slightly with the flow.

1 Man
Move forward on to the left foot, moving right behind the woman. (Count – slow)

3 Man
Step in place with the left foot, completing a 90° turn to the left. (Count – slow)

2 Man
Starting to turn to the left, move sideways on to the right foot (part weight). (a)

4 Man
Move forward on to the right foot, moving left behind the woman. (Count – slow)

1 Woman
Move forward on to the right foot, moving in front of the man. (Count – slow)

2 Woman
Starting to turn to the right, move sideways on to the left foot (part weight). (a)

3 Woman
Step in place with the right foot, completing a 90° turn to the right. (Count – slow)

4 Woman
Move forward on to the left foot, moving in front of the man. (Count – slow)

5 Man

Starting to turn to the right, move sideways on to the left foot (part weight). (a)

5 Woman

Starting to turn to the left, move sideways on to the right foot (part weight). (a)

Possible Combinations

• Side Samba Walk, Bota Fogos, Travelling Volta to the Right

• Travelling Volta to the Right, Bota Fogos (4–6, then 1–3), Travelling Volta to the Left.

Experimentation is half the fun of putting together your own routine, so have a go and enjoy it.

7–9 Man & Woman

Repeat Steps 1–3. (Count – slow a slow)

6 Man

Step in place with the right foot, completing a 90° turn to the right. (Count – slow)

6 Woman

Step in place with the left foot, completing a 90° turn to the left. (Count – slow)

Style Tip

If you have danced the Bota Fogos after the Side Samba Walk, you can now continue your routine by dancing the Travelling Volta to the Right.

Footwork

1. BF, 2. inside edge of toe, 3. BF, 4.BF, 5. inside edge of toe, 6. BF, 7. BF, 8. inside edge of toe, 9. BF

This figure can also be danced between the Travelling Volta to the Right and the Travelling Volta to the Left. In this case, start the Bota Fogos in Promenade Position at Step 4: dance Steps 4–6 and 1–3, then continue into the Travelling Volta to the Left.

Kick Change

Once you have danced the Travelling Volta to the Right, you can insert a fun figure into your Samba. The man is facing the centre line and is standing on the left foot which is crossed over the right foot. The woman is facing the wall and is standing on the right foot which is crossed over the left foot. The man retains a left hand to right hand hold with the woman.

1 Man
Move forward on to the right foot slightly to the left. (Count – slow)

1 Woman
Move forward on to the left foot slightly to the right. (Count – slow)

2 Man
Swaying a little to the left, kick the left foot forward from the knee. (Count – slow)

2 Woman
Swaying a little to the right, kick the right foot forward from the knee. (Count – slow)

3 Man
Move back on to the left foot. (Count – slow)

3 Woman
Move back on to the right foot. (Count – slow)

Footwork

1. BF, 2. Kick, 3. BF, 4. B, 5. BF

4 Man

Place the right foot behind the left foot (part weight). (a)

4 Woman

Place the left foot behind the right foot (part weight). (a)

Style Tip

It adds a stylish flair to this figure for the couple to touch free hands on Step 2, the kick. If, however, you find this move a little tricky at first, you can try substituting a simple tap behind with the right foot for the man and the left foot for the woman for Steps 4–5. The tap will have a count of Slow.

Review of Samba Routine

• Samba Whisk to the Right, Left and Right, ending in Promenade Position
• Left Foot Samba Walk, Right Foot Samba Walk, Left Foot Samba Walk
• Side Samba Walk
• Bota Fogos in Shadow Position
• Travelling Volta to the Right
• Kick Change, Kick Change
• Bota Fogos, Steps 4–6, 1–3 (optional)
• Travelling Volta to the Left
• Samba Whisk to the Left
• Start again

5 Man

Step in place with the left foot.
(Count – slow)

5 Woman

Step in place with the right foot.
(Count – slow)

Many dancers like to repeat this move before continuing into the Travelling Volta to the Left.

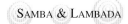

Samba Turns

While the man is dancing a Samba Whisk, the woman may enhance her move by dancing one of a number of turns. The woman turns to the right when the man is dancing the whisk to the left and she turns to the left when he is dancing the whisk to the right. Use the Samba Bounce Action when dancing this figure.

UNDERARM TURN TO THE RIGHT – *The woman dances this turn while the man is dancing the Samba Whisk to the Left. Start having just danced the Travelling Volta to the Left. The man is standing on the right foot, having crossed it in front of the left, and the woman is standing on the left foot, having crossed it in front of the right.*

1 Man
Move sideways on to the left foot (ball–flat), raising the left arm. (Count – slow)

1 Woman
Move sideways on to the right foot (ball–flat), crossing it in front of the left foot and starting to turn to the right under the man's raised arm. (Count – slow)

2 Man
Cross the right foot behind the left foot (Latin Cross, part weight). (a)

2 Woman
Move the left foot sideways and back (part weight), still turning to the right. (a)

3 Man
Step in place with the left foot (ball–flat), lowering the left arm. (Count – slow)

3 Woman
Cross the right foot in front of the left foot, continuing to turn to the right to face the man. (Count – slow)

Continue with a Samba Whisk to the Right and back into your routine.

UNDERARM TURN TO THE LEFT – *This turn is danced in the same way as the Underarm Turn to the Right, but this time with the man dancing a Samba Whisk to the Right and raising the left arm.*

1 Man

Move sideways on to the right foot, raising the left arm. (Count – slow)

3 Man

Step in place with the right foot, lowering the left arm. (Count – slow)

1 Woman

Move sideways on to the left foot, crossing it in front of the right foot and starting to turn to the left under the man's raised arm. (Count – slow)

2 Man

Cross the left foot behind the right foot. (part weight). (a)

2 Woman

Move the right foot sideways and back (part weight), still turning to the left. (a)

3 Woman

Cross the left foot in front of the right foot, continuing to turn to the left to face the man. (Count – slow)

Continue with a Samba Whisk to the Left and back into your routine.

Footwork

1. BF, 2. B, 3. BF

Foot Change Turn to the Left

Here is another linking move which will open the door to a number of very different and exciting dance-floor options. The woman dances only two steps while the man dances three. Her Step 1 is danced as the man dances his Steps 1 and 2. This move replaces the Underarm Turn to the Left.

Shadow Hold

In the Shadow Hold, the man is to the left and slightly behind the woman. Her left hand is in his left hand. Her right hand is extended to the side at roughly shoulder height, while the man's right hand moves to the woman's right shoulder-blade.

You can now make a metaphorical, though significant leap, using your existing routine. In the Shadow Hold, you can dance through your programme again, but this time with the woman dancing the same steps as the man as you retain the Shadow Hold.

As you dance in the Shadow Hold, it is important for the man to help position the woman and keep her in the same relative position to himself throughout the moves.

Man

Dance the Samba Whisk to the Right, raising the right arm and turning the figure 90° to the left to end facing with the flow. During the turn, release hold and take up a Shadow Hold on Step 3.

1 **Woman**
Move sideways onto the left foot (ball–flat), starting to turn to the left under the man's raised arm.
(Count – slow)

2 **Woman**
Continuing to turn to the left on the left foot, close the right foot to the left foot and end standing on the right foot, facing with the flow in Shadow Hold. (Count – slow)

FOOT CHANGE TURN FROM SHADOW TO CLOSE HOLD – *At the end of the Travelling Voltas in Shadow Hold, the man continues with a Samba Whisk to the Left. The woman, however, needs to revert to dancing using the opposite foot to the man. This is done very simply while the man dances his normal Samba Whisk to the Left. The man leads this figure by moving his left hand slightly to the left and exerting a little pressure on the woman's back with his right hand on the last step of the Volta, then moving his left hand to the right and across to indicate the turn to the woman on the "a" count of his Samba Whisk. The man then releases hold to allow the woman to turn.*

1 Woman

Move forward onto the left foot, starting to turn towards the man.
(Count – slow)

2 Woman

Close the right foot to the left foot, turning to end facing the man.
(Count – slow)

Review of Samba Routine including Shadow Hold

• Samba Whisk to the Right, Left and Right, ending in Promenade Position
• Left Foot Samba Walk, Right Foot Samba Walk, Left Foot Samba Walk
• Side Samba Walk
• Travelling Volta to the Right
• Kick Change, Kick Change
• Travelling Volta to the Left
• Samba Whisk to the Left (man), with Underarm Turn to the Right (woman)
• Samba Whisk to the Right (man), with Foot Change Turn to the Left (woman)
• Repeat the programme from the beginning in Shadow Hold, concluding with the Samba Whisk to the Left (man), with Foot Change Turn from Shadow to Close Hold (woman)
• Start again

Take up the normal Close Hold and continue with the Samba Whisk to the Right.

Samba Side Steps

Many Samba moves really come alive when you relax and enjoy the rhythm. The Samba Side Steps can be inserted into your programme after the Travelling Volta to the Left and before continuing into the Samba Whisk to the Left. The figure moves sideways along the room with the flow. The man starts by taking a Double Hand Hold, with his palms facing the woman and hands at shoulder height. The man is standing on the right foot facing the wall and the woman on the left foot facing the centre line.

1 Man
Move sideways on to the left foot. (Count – slow)

1 Woman
Move sideways on to the right foot. (Count – slow)

2 Man
Close the right foot to the left foot. (Count – slow)

2 Woman
Close the left foot to the right foot. (Count – slow)

3 Man
Move sideways on to the left foot. (Count – quick)

3 Woman
Move sideways on to the right foot. (Count – quick)

4 Man
Close the right foot to the left foot. (Count – quick)

4 Woman
Close the left foot to the right foot. (Count – quick)

5 Man & Woman
Repeat step 1 of Samba Side Step. (Count – slow)

Style Tip

The Samba Side Steps use a "Merengue" (pronounced may-ren-gay) action. This dance is typified by delaying the transfer of weight on to the foot you are moving until the other foot moves.

1 Place the foot in position with a little pressure on to the floor but do not transfer your weight just yet.

2 Transfer your weight on to the foot just moved and straighten the knee. Make the next step but without putting any weight on to the foot and holding the heel clear of the floor. Straighten the knee of the standing leg, allowing the other knee to move a little across the standing knee.

Use this action throughout the Samba Side Steps except for step 10.

6–9
Repeat steps 2–5. (Count – slow, slow, quick, quick)

10
Repeat step 2. (Count – slow)

Samba Side Steps with Turn

You can add further spice to the Samba Side Steps by introducing a turn for the woman on Steps 3–5. Dance Steps 1–2 of the Samba Side Steps, but with no Merengue action on Step 2, so that the man is standing fully on the right foot and the woman fully on the left foot. The man releases hold with the right hand and raises the left hand so that the woman can turn under it along the room, while the man continues to dance his normal Steps 3–5 with Merengue action. Resume a Double Hand Hold at the end of Step 5. It is crucial for the woman to remember that, throughout the turn, each step continues to progress along the room, so she should keep her feet apart and not turn back on herself.

5 Woman

Continuing to turn to the right, move sideways on to the right foot with the flow along the room to end facing the man. Resume a Double Hand Hold.
(Count – slow)

3 Woman

Move forward on to the right foot, turning to the right to face with the flow.
(Count – quick)

4 Woman

Move sideways on to the left foot with the flow along the room, continuing to turn to the right to end backing the man.
(Count – quick)

6–10 Woman

Dance the normal Samba Side Steps, resuming the Merengue action.

Contra Bota Fogos

The same type of movement as that of the classic Bota Fogos danced earlier can now be used in an interesting variation. In the Contra Bota Fogos, you will be dancing opposite your partner. Start having danced three Samba Walks, so that the man is standing on the left foot and the woman on the right foot, facing along the room with the flow. This move does not progress around the room. A slight Samba Bounce Action is used throughout the figure, but be careful not to exaggerate it. In the first part of the move, the man dances only two steps while the woman dances three. This enables the man to change feet ready for the Contra Bota Fogos.

PREPARATORY FOOT CHANGE ____

1 **Man**

Releasing hold with the right hand, point the right foot forward on a diagonal without putting any body weight on to it. (Count – slow)

1 **Woman**

Move forward a small step, on to the left foot, starting to turn to the left on to a diagonal facing the centre line of the room. (Count – slow)

2 **Man**

Taking up a Double Hand Hold, point the right foot back. (Count – slow)

2 **Woman**

Continuing to turn to the left, move sideways on to the right foot (part weight). (a)

3 **Woman**

Step in place with the left foot towards the centre line, completing a ⅜ turn to the left to end facing the man.

CONTRA BOTA FOGOS – *The steps for both the man and the woman are the same in this figure.*

1 Move forward a small step, on to the right foot. (Count – slow)

2 Turning to the right, move sid on to the left foot (part weight).

6 Step in place with the left foot, completing a 90° turn to the left. (Count – slow)

ep in place with the right foot, leting a 90° turn to the right. nt – slow)

love forward a small step, on to the foot. (Count – slow)

5 Turning to the left, move sideways on to the right foot (part weight). (a)

Footwork

1. BF, 2. Inside edge of toe, 3. BF, 4. BF, 5. Inside edge of toe, 6. BF

eps 1–6 of the Contra Bota Fogos may now be repeated.

Exit

Man

Repeat the Preparatory Foot Change, releasing hold with the right hand on the first step and resuming a hold appropriate to the next figure on the second step.

Woman

Repeat the Preparatory Contra Bota Fogos and resume a hold appropriate to the next figure as determined by the man.

Continuous Volta Turn

The same type of move as danced earlier in the easier Travelling Volta can now be used in a different pattern to dance a Continuous Volta Turn. The feel will be similar to that of the Travelling Voltas but the look will be surprisingly new and attractive. Unlike the Travelling Voltas, this move does not progress around the room. To get into position, dance the Preparatory Foot Change (man) and the Preparatory Bota Fogo (woman), as described previously, to start in the same position as for the Contra Bota Fogos. The man and woman are both standing on the left foot in a Double Hand Hold. The man dances a series of Voltas around the woman to end facing with the flow in a close Shadow Hold, with the woman on his left.

1 Man

Move the right foot across in front of the left foot (Latin Cross), curving clockwise around the woman. Move the right arm up and to the left to lead the woman to turn. (Count – slow – 1)

1 Woman

Move on to the right foot (Latin Cross), turning clockwise. (Count – slow – 1)

2 Man

Move the left foot sideways a small step, along the curve (part weight). Start to circle the right hand clockwise, but leave the left hand at waist height so that the woman starts to turn into it. (a)

2 Woman

Move the left foot sideways a small step (part weight), still turning clockwise. (a)

3 Man

Move the right foot across in front of the left foot along the curve (Latin Cross), still leading the woman to turn. (Count – slow – 2)

3 Woman

Move on to the right foot (Latin Cross), still turning clockwise. (Count – slow – 2)

4 Man

Move the left foot sideways a small step, along the curve (part weight), still leading the woman to turn. (a)

4 Woman

Move the left foot sideways a small step (part weight), still turning clockwise. (a)

5 Man

Move the right foot across in front of the left foot along the curve (Latin Cross), still leading the woman to turn. (Count – slow – 3)

5 Woman

Move on to the right foot (Latin Cross), still turning clockwise. (Count – slow – 3)

7 Man

Move the right foot across in front of the left foot along the curve (Latin Cross) to end facing with the flow. Lower the right hand to waist height. End in a close Shadow Hold with the woman on your left. (Count – slow – 4)

7 Woman

Turn into the man's left arm. Move on to the right foot (Latin Cross), still turning clockwise to end facing with the flow, in a close Shadow Hold with the man on your right. (Count – slow – 4)

6 Man

Move the left foot sideways a small step, along the curve (part weight), still leading the woman to turn. (a)

6 Woman

Move the left foot sideways a small step (part weight), still turning clockwise. (a)

Practical Tip

During the Continuous Volta Turn, the woman will turn around the ball of her right foot, which should remain in the same position on the floor. During Steps 1–6, the man will keep his right foot facing the woman.

Exit from Volta Turn

Retaining the close Shadow Hold, dance either two or four Samba Walks, both starting with the left foot.

On the final Samba Walk, the man should release hold with the right hand and dance a Side Samba Walk, following the woman's steps for the Side Samba Walk given earlier in the book, to a count of "Slow a Slow". The woman meanwhile should dance two forward walks: left foot, right foot (Count – slow, slow).

Continue with either the Bota Fogo in Shadow Position, starting with Step 4, or better still, the Travelling Volta to the Left, to end facing each other.

Samba Reggae

Samba Reggae is a fun variant of the Samba which even non-dancers can get straight into. This is a dance you can enjoy solo as there is no need for a partner. Coming from the Bahia region in the north-east of Brazil, the music is a cross between Samba and Reggae. With its vibrant and catchy beat it is a popular option for singles as well as a wider audience of Latin music and dance enthusiasts. The effect is not unlike an aerobics event, with the solo dancers facing front, either scattered randomly or in lines. In Brazil, open-air Samba Reggae can attract large crowds of participants, all following the moves of the leader. Now it's time to relax and get those hips moving with a short routine of typical moves.

PASSO BASICO – *This is the basic Samba Reggae move and is very similar to the Side Basic Samba but without the weight change. Start standing with your feet a little apart. Feel the rhythm and interpret it by adding your own expression to the basic move. Use the whole of your body to dance with the beat.*

1 Move sideways on to the left foot. (Count – slow)

2 Tap or touch the right foot next to the left foot. (Count – slow)

3 Move sideways on to the right foot. (Count – slow)

4 Tap or touch the left foot next to the right foot. (Count – slow)

Dance the Basic Samba Reggae four times.

PASSO DE MIKE TYSON – *This move includes the type of defensive shoulder shrug used by boxers like the world-class heavyweight champion Mike Tyson. Go to Bahia and everyone will know the Passo de Mike Tyson. There is no need to take steps in this move. Start with your feet apart, standing on your right foot.*

O PENTE – *Of course, everyone wants to make a good impression when out on the dance scene, and personal grooming and style is important. In this move, the dancers' movements resemble combing the hair, hence the name the "Comb". In O Pente, there are no steps, so your feet do not move. Start with your feet apart, standing on the right foot.*

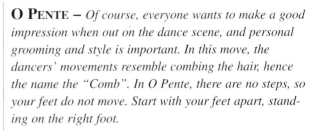

1 Transfer your body weight slowly on to the left foot, as you turn your upper body to the right. Draw your left hand over your head as if combing your hair. (Count – slow, slow)

1 Transfer your body weight on to the left foot and move the left shoulder forward, while making a fist with your hands. (Count – slow, slow)

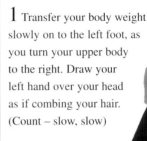

2 Transfer your body weight on to the right foot and move the right shoulder forward, while making a fist with your hands. (Count – slow, slow)

2 Transfer your body weight slowly on to the right foot, as you turn your upper body to the left. Draw your right hand over your head as if combing your hair. (Count – slow, slow)

ABRIR A CORTINA – *This means "Opening the Curtains". It is the same as the Passo Basico but with arm movements to mime opening the curtains.*

1 Move sideways on to the left foot, extending the left arm and moving it outwards to end opposite the left foot. Rest the right hand on the right hip. (Count – slow)

2 Tap or touch the right foot next to the left foot. (Count – slow)

3 Move sideways on to the right foot, extending the right arm and moving it outwards to end opposite the right foot. Rest the left hand on the left hip. (Count – slow)

4 Tap or touch the left foot next to the right foot. (Count – slow)

PASSO DE PELE – *Brazil is well known as a sport-loving nation, so it is not surprising that sporting heroes should be made a part of the other national pastime, dancing. Here, tribute is paid to one of Brazil's soccer superheroes in the "Pele Step".*

1 Move forward on to the left foot. (Count – slow)

2 Kick the right foot forward (as if kicking a football). (Count – slow)

3 Move back on to the right foot. (Count – slow)

4 Tap the left foot behind but without transferring your body weight. (Count – slow)

A BAILARINA – *This is the "Ballerina Step" and has a very similar pattern to that of the Samba Whisk described in the previous section of the book. During the move to the left, rotate the arms clockwise to end extended on the left side. During the move to the right, rotate the arms anticlockwise to end extended on the right side.*

1 Move sideways on to the left foot. (Count – slow)

2 Tap or touch the right foot behind the left foot, turning the right foot out. Avoid lowering the right heel but maintain pressure through the toes. (Count – slow)

3 Move sideways on to the right foot. (Count – slow)

4 Tap or touch the left foot behind the right foot, turning the left foot out. Avoid lowering the left heel but maintain pressure through the toes. (Count – slow)

You may choose instead to dance the Samba Whisk but with less bounce action than normal. Your timing would then be Slow a Slow, Slow a Slow. The six steps of the Samba Whisk take exactly the same time to dance as the four steps of the Bailarina, so you can interchange the moves as you wish.

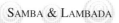

Lambada – an Introduction

The enduring popularity of a dance often ensures that certain of its characteristics will be adapted and developed to produce new and exciting variants. By 1987, a new variant of the Samba had burst on to the world dance scene – the Lambada. This new dance was a distillation of the northern Brazilian Forro, the Dominican Merengue and the Carimbo from Marajo, a dance in which the couple are in close contact with their legs intertwined. The name derives from the verb "lambar", which in northern Brazil means "heavy necking".

Originally, Lambada became popular mainly in the Para region of northern Brazil, until 1989, when an enterprising Frenchman introduced the dance to Paris and coupled it with the catchy music of the group Kaoma. The dance took Europe by storm and went on to become a world hit. In holiday resorts and clubs all over the world, hips were gyrating and hair was being flicked provocatively to the sensual pulse of the Lambada.

THE RHYTHM

Lambada is danced in sections, usually of three steps, to a count of "Slow, Quick, Quick" with the accent on the first count. The terms "Slow" and "Quick" are explained fully in the Music and Rhythm section of the Samba part of the book.

LAMBADA HOLD

The man places his right hand around the woman's waist to support her lower back while she places her left hand comfortably on the man's right shoulder. The man extends his left hand to the side and a little forward to a point midway between himself and the woman and takes the woman's right hand in his left hand at about chest height. On a crowded floor, the man should retract his left arm out of consideration for the other dancers. The inside of the man's and the woman's right legs should be touching sensuously just above the knee.

FITTING THE MOVES TOGETHER

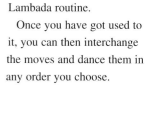

All the Lambada moves which follow start with the man's left foot and the woman's right foot and finish with the man's right foot and the woman's left. They all start in the same hold. In this way, the moves can be danced in any order, and you can have fun building up your own Lambada routine.

Once you have got used to it, you can then interchange the moves and dance them in any order you choose.

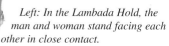

Left: In the Lambada Hold, the man and woman stand facing each other in close contact.

Basic Lambada

This move can be danced on the spot, in which case Step 2 will have only a very slight movement, or it can be danced with a forward and backward movement on Steps 2 and 3, as described here. Start by dancing the move on the spot and then, when you are ready, try introducing a little forward and backward movement. The man starts with his weight on the right foot and the woman with her weight on the left foot.

1 Man
Step in place with the left foot.
(Count – slow)

2 Man
Move diagonally forward on to the right foot, rolling your hips clockwise around the outside edge of your foot.
(Count – quick)

3 Man
Transfer your body weight on to the left foot.
(Count – quick)

3 Woman
Transfer your body weight on to the right foot.
(Count – quick)

1 Woman
Step in place with the right foot.
(Count – slow)

2 Woman
Move diagonally back on to the left foot, rolling your hips anticlockwise around the outside edge of your foot.
(Count – quick)

4 Man

Move the right foot back a small step.
(Count – slow)

4 Woman

Move the left foot forward a small step.
(Count – slow)

6 Man

Transfer your body weight on to the right foot. (Count – quick)

5 Man

Move diagonally back on to the left foot, rolling your hips anticlockwise around the outside edge of your foot. (Count – quick)

5 Woman

Move diagonally forward on to the right foot, rolling your hips clockwise around the outside edge of your foot. (Count – quick)

6 Woman

Transfer your body weight on to the left foot. (Count – quick)

Lambada Hip Roll

On Steps 2 and 5, both dancers roll their body weight around the edge of the foot. This is the famous Lambada hip roll. During the hip roll, there will be a little pressure where the man's and woman's right legs are in contact just above the knee.

Footwork

Generally, the man should use a ball to flat foot action but the woman should dance only on the balls of the feet and keep her legs straighter than the man to facilitate turns.

Swing Step

The Swing Step is a basic move but it is often used in combination with other moves and as part of the entry into some of the classic Lambada turns. Feel the swing through the hips as you get another chance to dance the raunchy Lambada hip roll. Start in the Lambada Hold described above and with your body weight on the same foot as before.

1 Man
Step in place with the left foot.
(Count – slow)

1 Woman
Step in place with the right foot.
(Count – slow)

2 Man
Move sideways on to the right foot with the clockwise Lambada hip roll, moving your right side forward.
(Count – quick)

2 Woman
Move sideways on to the left foot with the anticlockwise Lambada hip roll and moving your left side forward.
(Count – quick)

3 Man
Transfer your body weight on to the left foot, completing the Lambada hip roll and moving your right side back to its normal position.
(Count – quick)

3 Woman
Transfer your body weight on to the right foot, completing the Lambada hip roll and moving your left side back to its normal position. (Count – quick)

4 Man

Step in place with the right foot.
(Count – slow)

5 Man

Move sideways on to the left foot with the anticlockwise Lambada hip roll and moving your left side forward.
(Count – quick)

6 Man

Transfer your body weight on to the right foot, completing the Lambada hip roll and moving your left side back to its normal position. (Count – quick)

4 Woman

Step in place with the left foot.
(Count – slow)

5 Woman

Move sideways on to the right foot with the clockwise Lambada hip roll and moving your right side forward.
(Count – quick)

6 Woman

Transfer your body weight on to the left foot, completing the Lambada hip roll and moving your right side back to its normal position. (Count – quick)

Continue with any basic Lambada move.

Abrindo Portas

Abrindo Portas means "Sliding Doors" and is a combination of typical and exciting Lambada moves which are still relatively easy. If you work through the following steps steadily in sections, success will be yours. Start in the Lambada Hold described previously, with the man standing on the right foot and the woman on the left foot.

1 Man
Step in place with the left foot. (Count – slow)

2 Man
Move diagonally forward on to the right foot with the clockwise Lambada hip roll. (Count – quick)

3 Man
Transfer your body weight on to the left foot raising the left arm and leading the woman to start turning to the right underneath the joined hands. (Count – quick)

4 Man
Move sideways on to the right foot, turning the woman to her right underneath the joined hands. (Count – slow)

1 Woman
Step in place with the right foot. (Count – slow)

2 Woman
Move diagonally back on to the left foot with the anticlockwise Lambada hip roll. (Count – quick)

3 Woman
Move forward a small step, on to the right foot, starting to turn to the right underneath the man's raised arm. (Count – quick)

4 Woman
Move forward on to the left foot, continuing to turn to the right, away from the man underneath his raised arm. (Count – slow)

5 Man

Move diagonally forward on to the left foot, lowering the left hand to waist height. (Count – quick)

5 Woman

Move back on to the right foot, continuing to turn to end roughly parallel to the man. (Count – quick)

6 Man

Transfer your body weight back on to the right foot, leading the woman to start turning across you, then release hold. (Count – quick)

6 Woman

Transfer your body weight forward on to the left foot, starting to turn to the left across the man. The man will release hold. (Count – quick)

7 Man

Move sideways on to the left foot, allowing the woman to pass in front of you and taking her left hand in your right hand. (Count – slow)

7 Woman

Move sideways on to the right foot, passing in front of the man and continuing to turn to the left. Resume hold with the left hand. (Count – slow)

8 Man

Move diagonally forward on to the right foot, away from the woman. (Count – quick)

8 Woman

Move back on to the left foot, continuing to turn to face the man. (Count – quick)

9 Man

Transfer your body weight back on to the left foot, starting to lead the woman to pass in front of you. (Count – quick)

9 Woman

Transfer your body weight forward on to the right foot, preparing to pass in front of the man. (Count – quick)

10 Man

Move sideways on to the right foot, passing behind the woman and taking hold of her right hand in your left hand. (Count – slow)

10 Woman

Move sideways on to the left foot, passing in front of the man and changing from left hand to right hand hold. (Count – slow)

11 Man

Move diagonally forward and a little across yourself on to the left foot. (Count – quick)

11 Woman

Move back on to the right foot, continuing to turn to end roughly parallel to the man. (Count – quick)

12 Man

Transfer your body weight back on to the right foot, leading the woman to turn across you by raising the left hand and rotating her anticlockwise. (Count – quick)

12 Woman

Transfer your body weight forward on to the left foot, swivelling anticlockwise on the left foot to face the man. (Count – quick)

13 Man

Move back a small step, on to the left foot, resuming the normal Lambada hold. (Count – slow)

13 Woman

Move forward a small step, on to the right foot, between the man's feet. (Count – slow)

14 Man

Move diagonally forward on to the right foot, with the clockwise Lambada hip roll. (Count – quick)

14 Woman

Move diagonally back on to the left foot, with the anticlockwise Lambada hip roll. (Count – quick)

Continue with any basic Lambada move.

---

15 Man

Transfer your body weight back on to the left foot. (Count – quick)

15 Woman

Move forward a small step, on to the right foot. (Count – quick)

16–18 Man

Dance Steps 4–6 of the Basic Lambada. (Count – slow, quick, quick)

16–18 Woman

Dance Steps 4–6 of the Basic Lambada. (Count – slow, quick, quick)

Using Your Head

The woman's use of the head is crucial to looking her best when dancing the Lambada. While she will want to use her head in her own way to express both herself and the fluidity of the movement, there are a few useful guidelines to follow.

• All head movements are a natural extension of the move being danced.

• In the normal Lambada hold, the woman does not look at the man.

• The woman looks at the man only at the start and finish of each move.

• If the woman is behind the man or in front of him with her back to him, she may look at him.

Above: The woman begins and ends each move with her head inclined to the side.

Above: To move her head from left to right, the woman will roll it, circling it across with chin down.

Above: To move her head from right to left, she will roll it, circling it across with chin up.

Basic Lambada Turns

You can now try spicing up your Lambada with some exciting turns. This group of moves is complete in itself, so you can include it in your programme as soon as you have had a little practice. Start by dancing Steps 1–3 of the Basic Lambada, but on Step 2, the man should indicate his intention to dance the turns by turning his body a little to the left as he steps forward.

MAN'S SWING STEP TO THE LEFT – *The woman will open out during this move.*

4 Man

Step in place with the right foot.
(Count – slow)

5 Man

Move sideways on to the left foot with the anticlockwise Lambada hip roll and turning your upper body to the right.
(Count – quick)

6 Man

Transfer your body weight on to the right foot, completing the Lambada hip roll and turning your upper body to the left to resume its normal position.
(Count – quick)

4 Woman

Move forward a small step, on to the left foot. (Count – slow)

5 Woman

Pivoting on the ball of the left foot, make almost a half turn to the right to end on the man's right side and step back on to the right foot. (Count – quick)

6 Woman

Transfer your body weight forward on to the left foot, starting to turn to the left.
(Count – quick)

MAN'S SWING STEP TO THE RIGHT – *As before the woman will open out.*

7 Man
Close the left foot almost to the right foot, leading the woman to turn square to you. (Count – slow)

8 Man
Move sideways on to the right foot, keeping your body weight between your feet and turning your upper body to the left to lead the woman to continue turning anticlockwise. (Count – quick)

9 Man
Transfer your body weight fully on to the left foot, leading the woman to start her turn to the right. (Count – quick)

9 Woman
Transfer your body weight forward on to the right foot, starting to turn to the right. (Count – quick)

7 Woman
Move sideways on to the right foot to end facing the man square on. (Count – slow)

8 Woman
Pivoting on the ball of the right foot, make almost a half turn to the left to end on the man's left side and step back (part weight) on to the left foot. (Count – quick)

Continue with the Basic Lambada.

BAILARINA WITH UNDERARM TURN – *The man prepares to turn the woman while she executes a Bailarina turn.*

10 Man
Close the right foot to the left foot, leading the woman to turn square to you. (Count – slow)

11 Man
Move sideways on to the left foot, with the anticlockwise Lambada hip roll and turning your upper body to the right. (Count – quick)

Pivot

A pivot is a turn made on only one foot. As you pivot, both legs will be straight but you will be standing on only the left foot. During the pivot, it is important to allow the right foot to close naturally to the left foot, so that you pivot with both feet under the body. This will not only give you better balance but will also allow the right foot to end in the best position to continue into the next move.

12 Man
Transfer your body weight on to the right foot, completing the Lambada hip roll and turning the woman to the left, across you and underneath your raised left arm to end facing each other. (Count – quick)

10 Woman
Move sideways on to the left foot, turning to the right to end facing the man square on. (Count – slow)

11 Woman
Pivoting on the ball of the left foot, make almost a half turn to the right to end on the man's right side and step back on to the right foot. (Count – quick)

12 Woman
Transfer your body weight forward and pivot on the left foot, turning to the left underneath the man's raised arm to end facing him. (Count – quick)

A Cadeira

The name of this classic Lambada move means "The Seat" in Portuguese, although it has now become so popular with photographers that it is sometimes called "The Photo" instead. In this move, the man leads the woman to a position in which she appears to be momentarily sitting on his knee.

1 Man

Move sideways on to the left foot, leading the woman to open out to your right. (Count – slow)

2 Man

Transfer your body weight on to the right foot, leading the woman to turn to the left towards you. (Count – quick)

3 Man

Move the left foot forward without any weight. (Count – quick)

1 Woman

Swivelling a half turn on the left foot, move back on to the right foot. (Count – slow)

2 Woman

Transfer your body weight forward on to the left foot, starting to turn to the left. (Count – quick)

3 Woman

Move forward across the man on to the right foot. (Count – quick)

4 Man

Hold the foot position.
(Count – slow)

4 Woman

With the feet in place,
swivel a half turn to
the left to end on the
right foot with the man
on your right.
(Count – slow)

5 Man

Press the ball of the left foot down on the
floor but do not lower the heel, raising
the left knee as you lower through the
right knee. Raising the left arm, continue
to turn the woman, allowing her to lower
on to your left knee.
(Count – quick)

6 Man

Stand up and close the left foot back to
the right foot, leading the woman to face
you and resuming the normal Lambada
hold. (Count – quick)

5 Woman

Flex the right knee and lift the left foot
to the outside of the right knee to create
the illusion that you are sitting on the
man's knee. (Count – quick)

6 Woman

Stand up and turn to the right to face the
man, ending with your weight on the
right foot. (Count – quick)

Continue with any of the Lambada moves you have learned.

Lambada Drop

The Drop is an exotic and effective move which has justifiably become the trademark of the Lambada. In this move, the man holds his position while leading the woman to perform a body ripple which culminates in a flick of the hair. It is precisely for this purpose that dedicated female dancers grow their hair long to maximize and enhance the effect.

1 Man
Move forward a small step on to the left foot. (Count – slow)

1 Woman
Move back a small step on to the right foot. (Count – slow)

2 Man
Move diagonally forward on to the right foot, with the Lambada hip roll. (Count – quick)

2 Woman
Move diagonally back on to the left foot, with the Lambada hip roll. (Count – quick)

3 Man
Transfer your body weight back on to the left foot, leaving the right foot in place with the right knee slightly raised. Use the quick transfer of weight to bring the woman towards you to ensure close contact. (Count – quick)

3 Woman
Transfer your body weight forward on to the right foot and, pulled by the man, move the left foot close to the right foot, sandwiching the man's right knee between your legs. (If the man does not support your back properly, you many need to grip with your knees.) (Count – quick)

4–6 Man
As the woman performs her body ripple, hold your position and support the woman's lower back with your right hand, but do not restrict her movement. (Count – slow, quick, quick)

4–6 Woman
To perform your body ripple, contract your waist, inclining your upper body slightly forward and bending your knees. Bend backwards, pushing your hips forward. Progressively accelerate the roll of your back forward to resume the normal body position, straightening your knees and finishing with a flick of your hair. (Count – slow, quick, quick)

Continue with Steps 4–6 of the Basic Lambada, with the man moving the right foot back to the left foot on Step 4.

La Macarena

And now for a bonus dance. In 1996, a piece of Samba music captured the imagination of the world, reaching the number one position in the popular music charts of many countries. It was called "La Macarena" and one of the best versions was by a group called Los Del Rio. A special line dance was devised for this mega-hit and became the International Dance of the Year 1996. In the Macarena, the dancers arrange themselves either in lines facing front or in a circle facing centre. Everyone starts together and performs the same sequence of moves, one for the first beat of each new bar of music. Stand with your feet a little apart and just go with the music.

1 Extend the right arm, palm down.

2 Extend the left arm, palm down.

3 Turn the right hand palm up.

4 Turn the left hand palm up.

5 Move the right hand across to the left shoulder.

6 Move the left hand across to the right shoulder.

7 Move the right hand behind your head.

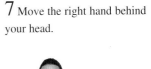

8 Move the left hand behind your head.

9 Move the right hand across to the left hip.

10 Move the left hand across to the right hip.

11 Move the right hand on to the right hip.

12 Move the left hand on to the left hip.

13 Roll your hips round to the right.

14 Roll your hips round to the left.

15 Clap.

16 Jump, making a quarter turn to the right.

Then, simply start again. A shorter version of the Macarena uses only moves 1, 2, 7, 8, 11, 12, 13 and 16. In some clubs, the turn is made to the left. Whichever version your club uses, get on to the floor and have some serious fun with the Macarena.

Music Suggestions

SAMBA

Many of the hits by the Brazilian artist Beto Barbosa are truly excellent Sambas. Try "Preta", "Souvenir" and "Do Re Mi Fa Sou Eu", from the album *Beto Barbosa* on the Gel Continental label.

"Não Sei, Não Sei", by Alipio Martins, is a great Samba, played at a faster pace for more expert dancers, but if you remember to keep your steps small, you can enjoy this track as a beginner.

For the type of music used in international and world-class competitions, choose recordings by Ross Mitchell and His Orchestra (UK), Günter Noris and His Orchestra (Germany), Klaus Hallen and His Orchestra (Germany) or Werner Tauber and His Orchestra (Germany). Most internationally accredited dance teachers will be able to advise you further and will often be able to order your requirements from specialist suppliers.

SAMBA REGGAE

You can dance Samba Reggae to almost any modern disco-type dance music, but if you want the authentic flavour, try the fabulous "Forreggae", by Beto Barbosa, or "Balanço do Merengue", by Papa Leguas.

You can enjoy dancing Samba Reggae at a slower pace to "Brilho Jamaica" by Laranja Mecânica.

LAMBADA

The world hit "Lambada", performed by the group Kaoma, is the original classic for Lambada dancers.

Beto Barbosa is a favourite artist, as he captures not only the superb rhythm but also a fabulous atmosphere in all his dance music. "Mar de Emocões" is one of his best.

"Dançando Lambada", performed by Avatar, was also an international Lambada hit, becoming almost as well known as Kaoma's "Lambada".

"Lambada do Galo Gago", by Getto Dougllas, is a popular number, oozing the rhythm and atmosphere of a tropical dance party in Rio or Bahia.

Further Information

It is to be hoped that this introduction has given you a taste of the Samba and Lambada and has whetted your appetite to learn more of the fascinating dances and rhythms from Latin America. With the moves you have learned in this book, you will soon be out on the floor dancing and enjoying the Samba and Lambada. Why not join others who share your interest? Look up your local dance school or call a Latin club in your area. Your teacher will be able to give you personal guidance to help you refine your technique and you will be surprised by how quickly you progress. Remember that most people find dancing a little difficult at first but, given a little time, patience and practice, you will soon have learned to dance, which is a lifetime's reward for such a little investment.

ACKNOWLEDGEMENTS

Many of the photographic sequences in this book feature UK Professional Latin-American Champions and world-class dancers, Goran and Nichola Nordin, whose help we gratefully acknowledge. We would also like to thank the Brazilian dancer Karina Rebello for her contribution and insights into the authentic detail of Lambada and Samba Reggae and to thank the following for their participation in the photography of this book: Luís Bittencourt, Berg Dias, Tanya Janes and Mina di Placido. Their expertise and enthusiasm were invaluable.